THE WORD

A Poetry Connection

Arnita L. Fields

Holy Poetry Publications

© 2008 by Arnita L. Fields
All rights reserved. No part of this book may be reproduced in any form without permission in writing from the publisher or author, except for brief quotes used in reviews.

First printing

All scripture references are from the New King James Version of the bible. Copyright © 1985 Thomas Nelson Publishers, Inc. Used by permission. All rights reserved.

ISBN: 978-0-578-00045-9
Published By Holy Poetry Publications
www.holypoetrypublications.net
Memphis, TN

Printed in the United States of America

Word of Thanks

GOD my Heavenly Father, who is my strong tower, refuge, my fortress and deliverer

My husband Anthony, a man after God's own heart

Etta O'Bryant (my mom), Diana Smith (my sister) and Shaunda Turner (my friend) for their assistance and prayers

To those in the body of Christ who share a love for God's word and who also desire to live more than just a mediocre Christian life

Special Dedication

To my special daughter Jasmine, your father introduced me to you after he and I met in 1997, although you were only 5 years old, I knew immediately that you would have a special place in my heart. Now, as your senior year in high school quickly approaches, I stop and reflect on the times we spent together and wonder if I have had enough opportunity to pour into you what God had required of me to do. With this thought in mind, I now leave you with a few words of wisdom as you prepare for a new chapter to unfold in your life.

1) Keep the word of God before your eyes, hide the word within your heart and allow God to lead you into His divine purpose.

2) Take time daily to fellowship with God, alone. Spend time listening for His voice, wait to see what He has to say to you.

3) Sing praises unto God daily, and always keep a spiritual song in your heart.

Love, Always

Introduction

The poems assembled in this collection were written in 2006 during a season of transition. I found myself once again in a place where God was downloading continuous instruction and revelation. The wisdom I received from the word of God helped to move me forth into the next level God was taking me to. When I was directed to write these poems, I was truly empty of myself. I had been allowing God's word to consume me as I meditated and prayed daily. My vessel was being purged at this time so I could readily receive the new plans of God that were being birthed forth in the spirit.

The word of God is indeed powerful and sharper than any two edged sword. Spend some time marinating and let the word of God help to change you into the vessel that God has ordained you to become.

May the anointing and healing power of the Lord be upon you, as you receive His instruction and wisdom from this poetry collection. So relax, free your mind and humble your heart as you allow the poetic word to minister to the very depths of your spirit.

Many Blessings,

Arnita L. Fields

God First Before All
Matthew 6:33

Don't try to seek me for the things that I do.

I know your heart because I AM the one that created you.

I AM the one who was there, before you were formed
in your mother's womb.

I sent my only son into the earth, so you could escape its dark
gloom.

Come after me with all of your heart, putting me as first in
your life, will be a very good start.

Pant hard after me, and you will definitely see,
I AM the God of more than enough who shall supply all of
your need.

Follow Me
Matthew 4:18-20

Leave behind your past and come follow me.
Follow me, follow me.

Cast your cares aside, come follow me.
Follow me, follow me.

I have what you need, come follow me.
Follow me, follow me.

I'll show you a new life, come follow me.
Follow me, follow me.

You can begin anew, come follow me.
Follow me, follow me.

Submit to me your life, come follow me.
Follow me, follow me.

Everything will be alright, if you follow me.
Follow me, follow me.

Preach God's Word
2 Timothy 4:2

Study God's word to show yourself approved,
so that you will not be made ashamed.

Study God's word, meditate upon His word, believe and it
won't all be done in vain.

Stay prepared at all times, keep His word flowing continually
through out your mind.

Keep His word hidden in your heart, and when your season
comes, it will easily flow out.

Preach His word without playing any games,
in boldness and clarity as you glorify God's Holy name.

Obey Me
Deuteronomy 28:1-2

Relinquish your will; forsake all of your ways.
Come hither to me and obey.

I created you and knew you before you were born.
I have been right there beside you through each and every storm.

There is wisdom, understanding and clarity in my will.
I AM all that you need, sit tight, be still.

Stop going here and running over there, can't you see my child; that I'm the one who cares?

I AM your father, let me lead you, let me mold you, let me teach you.

Submit to and obey me, so you can live.

Peculiar People
1 Peter 2: 9 (KJV)

A chosen generation, a royal priesthood, a holy nation called by God.

A peculiar people, a special people called out from within the dark.

We're no longer a part of this fleshly world, but called, chosen and set apart.

Redeemed, delivered and set free by the hands of a loving God.

Created to praise, honor, and worship and obey the Holy One.

We are brought out and set free from the curse of the law by Jesus Christ, God's only Son.

Live in My Presence
Exodus 33:13-15

Enter into my secret place, come into my heart and stay always.

Bask in my presence and receive my joy, make me your hearts desire and nothing more.

I have what you need when you stay with me.

I am your living Father and you will see, I will fill that void down in your soul.

Nothing else will take my place, because I AM the one who created in you that space.

Come live in my presence and you will see, I'm everything you have been searching for and the only one who can give you sweet, sweet peace.

Clean Heart
(Spiritual Song)
Psalm 51

Create in me a clean heart. Create in me a clean heart o God, o God.

Draw me to thee and set me free. Draw me to thee and set me free, o God, o God.

Send me your grace and your mercy. Send me your grace and your mercy, o God, o God.

Wash me, cleanse me, love and restore me. Wash me, cleanse me, love and restore me, o God, o God.

The Essence of Time
Ecclesiastes 3

Tick tock goes the clock.

It always goes forward and never goes back.

(Time waits for no one)

Capture the essence of every second, minute, hour and day.

Because once it's gone, it's gone.

(Time waits for no one)

There's a time and season for everything under the sun.

Know what time of the day you are in because,

(Time waits for no one)

Pray Without Ceasing
1 Thessalonians 5:17

In the morning, noon day and in the evening light,

A prayer upon your heart may help to save someone's life.

No matter the day or the hour at hand, prayer is always needed with so much pestilence across the land.

Pray for your own life and for others too.

Keep a prayer shield daily over your children while they are attending school.

Pray, pray, pray without ceasing.

Be Holy for I Am Holy
1 Peter 1:13-16

Clean speech, clean thoughts.

Clean heart, clean walk.

Holiness

Pure motives, pure love.

Pure desires, pure life.

Holiness

Live as Jesus lived.

Talk as Jesus talked.

Walk as Jesus walked.

Make your house a holy house.

Be holy, for I AM holy.

Bear Good Fruit
Galatians 5:16-26

How can a tree bear good fruit?

Hook your roots into the right water source.

Get in tune with God's plans and you'll stay right on course.

Let God prune you, when He sees that there is a need.

Live a life that honors Him and then good fruit will soon

fill up your tree.

Reverence Me
Hebrew 12:28

Honor, Respect, Adoration and Love,

are some of the elements befitting our God up above.

Give God the glory that is due unto His name.

Reverence the God who made the heavens and the earth,

He is the one who completed all of the work.

Submit your life unto God always.

Worship, praise Him and glorify His name.

In the center of God's presence we are

forever changed.

Humble Thyself
(Die Flesh Die)
James 4:7-10

Humble, humble, humble thyself, under the

mighty hand of God.

Trusting, trusting, and trusting, no matter how hard.

Stay below the radar and out of harm's way,

submit your life to God each and every day.

Die to the flesh and beat it way down.

It will lead you to a life of victory,

where you are no longer bound.

Meditate on These Things
Philippians 4:8

Meditate on things that are true,
'El Shaddai-God Almighty

Meditate on things that are honest,
'El Roi-The God who sees

Meditate on things that are just,
Tsidekenu-The Lord our Righteousness

Meditate on things that are pure,
Qedosh Yisra'el-The Holy One of Israel

Meditate on things that are lovely,
'El 'Elyon- God Most High

Meditate on things that are of a good report,
'El Rohi-The Lord is my shepherd

Have you Considered My Servant?
Job 1

Have you considered my servant, the one who called on my name, who relinquished their rights and stopped playing games?

Have you considered my servant, who came out of fiery trials, who would not give up or the one who did not drown?

This servant is the one, who was saved by my Grace, the one who now takes time out to seek my face.

This servant is the one who hears me when I call out his name, to give him sound wisdom and instruction as he faces each brand new day.

This is my servant, in whom I am well pleased.

Believe My Report
Numbers 13:31-33

Cast down the vain imaginations and lose all of your fears.

Stop all of your crying now, and clean out your spiritual ears.

There is great news for you, and yes, the story has been told before.

If I open a door up for you, there's no man that can shut that door.

I am the God who always gives His children a way of escape.

You even have a choice after all of the bad decisions that you make.

Believe my report. It's the one that you need to receive.

It will make your life much sweeter, but it is you who has to truly believe.

Complete the Work
Nehemiah 4

Don't stop the work for which I called you to do.

Don't abort your mission because others are distracting you.

Make up in your mind that no matter the cost, the Lord your God has chosen you and nothing will be lost.

Refocus your thoughts on the task at hand, and if you need help so that you can faithfully stand.

Surround yourself with people, the ones with a renewed heart, mind and soul, you will have a better chance to succeed and quickly complete your goal.

Your Time is it in My Hands?
Psalm 31:15

I formed you and I knew you from far back in time.

I am the Lord God, creator of all things. I am yours and you are mine.

If you give me a second, a minute or an hour of your day, the results you are looking for will be measured back to you in the same way.

Don't just give me your money, it's some of your time that I need.

I have wisdom, instruction, clarity and direction and your hungry soul to feed.

How much time do you have?

It's up to you!

New You
Isaiah 43:18-19

Let me cleanse you, and replace you back on my potter's wheel.

Let me smooth out all of the cracks and mend your bruised ego too.

Now, do not remember the former things, and all that has happened to you.

Give yourself a chance to dry out for a few more days.

Then you will be able to see a brand new you, as you reflect on life in your new clay.

A Godly Wife
Proverbs 31

You are a woman of substance, of wisdom, love and God's grace.

You are an upright woman, who values her place.

A woman not out, just seeking for some attention, but one who takes the time out to take care of her business.

A Proverbs 31 woman loves and cherishes her family.

She makes sure that she keeps herself spiritually aligned, so that she is able to meet the needs of her family each and every time.

No Weapon Formed
Isaiah 54:17

I am God and I know all things.

Nothing evil will remain hidden once my presence hits the scene.

No weapon formed against you will be able to prosper.

Get up put on your whole armor, and don't forget the sword of my word.

No enemy will be able to withstand you as you walk in the name of Jesus my Son, you will come out of your battle stronger and wiser then when you first begun.

The Blessing of the Lord
Proverbs 10:22

When you are blessed by God, there's no need to beg, steal or borrow.

His blessings make one rich and it adds no sorrow.

Every good and perfect gift comes down from the Father of lights.

They come more steadily when you honor God with your whole life.

The blessings of the Lord are for those in whom the Lord is well pleased.

If you seek after God first, your blessings will soon overtake thee.

Nobody but Jesus
Psalm 23

Nobody but Jesus could care for me so much.

He's the king of kings and the hope of glory and the Savior of my soul.

He's a living and righteous ruler and the lifter up of my head.

He's the only begotten of the Father and my living bread.

He's my strength in the time of sorrow and always meets my need.

He's the living word, Emmanuel and the faithful Prince of Peace.

Nobody but Jesus could love me after all the sacrifices He's made.

He's my Savior, redeemer and good shepherd in every possible way.

There's nobody but Jesus.

All of God and None of Me
Matthew 26:39

God I surrender my mind, my body and my soul to you.

I offer my hands, my feet, and my heart to you.

I surrender my fears, my tears, and my cares to you too.

I surrender my all to you.

Do with me God what you will, have your way as I try to keep still.

All of God and none of me,
in the center of your presence is where I desire to be.

I want to be full of God down to my very core, just basking in His presence, now and evermore.

Trust in the Lord
Proverbs 3:5

Trust in the Lord with all of your heart,

for God is the one who gave you your start.

Trust in the Lord and never doubt.

Kick fear to the door and lock it out.

Straight Path
Luke 13:24-28

There's only one way to Jesus, yes, He's the only path you will need.

Nothing else can save you, there's no other way to be free.

Dead works will not keep you, nor will playing any games.

The path is straight and narrow and for all it's the same.

God's Love
John 3:16

Love is really a splendid thing, there's much more to it than what the world thinks.

It involves sacrifice and not having one's way.

It's something that should be renewed each and everyday.

Love is beautiful and should be for always, it is evident in the love God has for us with the sacrifice He made.

Everlasting Love
Jeremiah 31:3

A love unlike no other, before we were formed in the womb,

a love that's real, it is the kind of love not based on just a good feel.

It's an everlasting love straight from the Father's heart.

A love without an ending, it's a love that will never stop.

Love your Enemies
Matthew 5:44

Love your enemies as I have loved you.

Forgive them for any trespass made against you.

Hold them up in prayer, as you call out to me their names.

Bless them in the name of Jesus, now and once again.

Delight Yourself in the Lord
Psalm 37:4

Come set your sights on the Love of your life.

Seek to get to know me more both during the day and the night.

Spend quality time with me when you are free.

With me as the love of your life, your soul will never be in need.

Hear His Voice
John 10:27

Shhhhhh!

Quiet your mind, calm your thoughts

believe in every word that my Son has

said and has taught.

Yes, Jesus is the key for you to be free.

He is in fact the mediator that stands

between you and me.

Hear His voice and live.

No Idols
Exodus 20:3

Nothing should ever come before me, because it will not be able to stand.

I am the God of Abraham, Isaac and Jacob,
I am the creator of all men.

Put down every idol and release now your hold.

I should always be the first in your life and the lover of your soul.

Wisdom One
Proverbs 2

Walk in my wisdom and forsake all of your ways.

Don't allow your flesh to pull you to where you disobey.

Walk in my wisdom and seek to understand my ways.

It will bring life to your body, and help to lengthen your days.

Guard Your Heart
Proverbs 4:20-27

Keep guard over your heart and don't abandon your post.

Be careful of who and what you entertain, for you are the host.

Guard your heart, so that you can remain free, from every vile and wicked deceptive trap of the enemy.

Forget not My Benefits
Psalm 103

Forget not all of my benefits. Forget not all of my ways.

Continue to offer up praise and thanksgiving unto my mighty name.

I am your God, who called you into my marvelous light.

I am the one who feeds you my goodness every morning, noon and night.

Continue to praise and honor me as I supply all of your need.

Mercy, grace and forgiveness your hungry soul I will feed.

Bridge of Restoration
James 5:19-20

Stand in the gap and take the lead, intercede for the backsliders so that they can be free.

Stand in the gap and show them the way, to a restored life and to a brighter day.

Stand in the gap with an outstretched hand, and lead men back to Christ and into my arms again.

Run with Patience
Hebrews 12:1-2

You see the road up ahead, and it seems like it could run on for miles and miles.

Should you slow down or quit the race or try to cover more ground?

What do you believe in? What has brought you here?

What do you have clinging to you to bring about all of these fears?

Take your eyes and focus them back on God's master plan.

Run with patience the race that is set before you, because only the faithful will be able to win.

Tear Keeper
Psalm 56:8

There are tears of joy and tears of pain.

Tears flowing from your eyes but they can never return again.

There are tears of hurt, tears of sorrow.

They are here today and gone tomorrow.

Tears, tears like a river, where do they flow?

Into a bottle up in heaven is where I am told.

Sing a New Song
Psalm 33:1-2

Come before the Father. Praise and bless His name.

Give Him the honor for each and every day.

Break forth in gladness, singing Ha-lle-lu.

Be grateful for a Father who takes good care of you.

He's worthy of the honor, and worthy of the praise.

Now and forever, we will bless His holy name.

Holy House
Psalm 101

Rid your home of all the things not like me.

Consider the things too, that you watch on TV.

Clean out your home each and every square.

Holiness begins in the home or don't you even care?

Make your home a holy house, forsaking all that

is evil, and putting the devil completely out.

Don't Fret Yourself
Psalm 37:1-2

Don't waste your time, don't you worry about a thing.

Don't even be concerned about the enemy and the trouble he brings.

Wait on God and He will see you through.

You'll come out victorious and there won't be anything that

the enemy can do to you.

God is on your side as you continue to take a stand.

And the workers of iniquity will soon be scattered far and wide, as the many grains of sand.

Lift up your Eyes
Psalm 121

Look to me and you will see I am the God

that helps to keep you free.

I never sleep, no not even a wink,

but I am by your side every day of the week.

Lift up your eyes unto my holy hill.

Cry out unto me and I will definitely hear.

I am always with you through the storms of your life,

and I will deliver you once again, by my power and my might.

I have the Plans
Jeremiah 29:11

You've been grasping for straws in the sea of life, running here and running there with all of your might.

Looking to Bobby and to Betty Sue, seeking out people, to see what they can do for you.

Shut down your project and come seek after me, I am the one who loves you and have come to set you free.

I have great plans that pertain to your life.

I am the one who holds the puzzle pieces and can set them in place upright.

I know the plans that I have for you, and I have the directions and the map, that will help to see you through.

Instruction from the Lord
Matthew 28:18-20

I sent my son into the world as a living sacrifice.

He was the living word made flesh as His presence illuminated the night.

Jesus, gathered 12 disciples and made them fishers of men.

Many others came and tagged along over the course of 3 years.

After Jesus' resurrection, up from the grave, he gathered His disciples together again, to declare a brand new day.

Go make disciples of the nations, and teach them all of my ways.

Then baptize them in the name of the Father, Son and Holy Ghost after they have been saved.

Abide in My Love
John 15:9

If you are looking for a love that will last always

If you are looking for a love that will brighten your day

If you are looking for a love that will make you weak in the knees

If you are looking for a love that would help to meet your needs.

There is a love that is stronger than steel.

There is a love not bound by your will.

There is a love that's oh so real, it's the unconditional love of God, now that's a true thrill!

Try it, you'll be hooked forever.

The Wedding Feast
Rev. 19:6-9

Here you will see beautiful china set all in place,

with gorgeous linen napkins lay carefully upon each plate.

There are thousands of tables lined up, many rows upon rows.

How many will be coming? Only our God truly knows.

The bridegroom has been ready for over 2000 years. He has waited ever so patiently for His bride to overcome her fears.

O what a celebration, a mighty time it will be, as the bride of Christ unites together as one with Christ at the lead.

Do Not Grieve the Holy Spirit
Ephesians 4:25-32

The Holy Spirit is a helper and a comforter to those who are saved.

He receives counsel from God to help show people a better way.

The Holy Spirit is real and He is your guide. He's here to help lead you to a holy life.

Hear what the spirit of God is saying to you.

Do your best, stop grieving the spirit of the almighty God and putting it to an unnecessary test.

Live to God's Will
1 Peter 4:1-3

Cease from sin, no longer try to have your way.

Come up out of darkness and choose the light of day.

Die to your flesh daily and push all of your ways aside.

Submit yourself to live to God's will or face

death in your own spiritual life.

Seeking God
2 Chronicles 7:14

Humble, Pray, Seek, And Turn.

Humble, Pray, Seek, And Turn.

Humble, Pray, Seek, And Turn.

Humble, Pray, Seek, And Turn.

    Receive

Return Unto the Lord
Isaiah 55:7

Leave behind your past, do it today.

Seek the Lord for it is now time to do things His way.

Awake out of your slumber, shake off your sleep.

Forsake all that is evil and rejoin the other sheep.

Prayer of Salvation

If after reading this book, you have a desire to know Jesus as your personal Lord and Savior, please take a moment to pray the following prayer:

I repent of all of my sins and right now, I do confess that Jesus is the Son of God. I believe that Jesus died and was buried and rose again, and is now seated at the right hand of God in Heaven. I receive Him now as Lord of my life and I commit to serve him for the rest of my days.
It is in the name of Jesus I do pray, Amen

If you have just prayed this prayer and want more information about beginning your new life as a Christian, please call or write us, we will be happy to send you a free booklet.

Holy Poetry Publications
6037 Blackwing Dr. Suite 171
Memphis, TN 38115
Email: arnitafields@yahoo.com
info@holypoetrypublications.net
Website: www@holypoetrypublications.net
Phone: (901) 786-3519

Other books by author Arnita L. Fields

Rescued, Restored, Renewed and Revived
A Collection of Christian Poems

And the Beat Goes On
Includes Poems from a Restored Marriage

This Far By Faith
Anthology
(Contributing Author)

America's Change
A Poetic View
(Coming January 2009)

Holy Poetry
Flowing thru my mind
(Coming June 2009)

Poet, writer and author, Arnita L. Fields is also a minister of the gospel who teaches the word of God with clarity and simplicity. She has a burning passion and desire to see that all marriages in the body of Christ operate and function in the divine order of God. Arnita is a government employee and also a full time student at Liberty University pursuing a degree in Psychology. She has a future goal of counseling troubled marriages. Arnita has been married to her husband Anthony for more than eleven years.

Contact Information

www.holypoetrypublications.net
www.myspace.com/arnita_fields
arnitafields@yahoo.com
901.786.3519

To schedule Arnita L. Fields for your next ministry event please use the contact information listed above. To schedule Arnita for your next literary event, you may contact Sherita Redic at (901) 643-9714 or by email info@sredicpublicity.net

www.ingramcontent.com/pod-product-compliance
Lightning Source LLC
Chambersburg PA
CBHW031432040426
42444CB00006B/771